Deeper Reflections *of* Life

Words to inspire the heart & uplift the soul

Stacey Ann Berry

Copyright © 2018 Stacey Ann Berry

All rights reserved. No part of this work, covered by the copyright herein, may be reproduced or used in any form or by any means—graphic, electronic, or mechanical, including photocopying, recording, taping or on information storage and retrieval systems without the prior permission of the author, except for inclusion in brief reviews with due credit given to the author.

Cover image: © Shutterstock

Design elements: Created by Freepik (vintage)

ISBN: 978-1-926926-93-3 (pbk)

ISBN: 978-1-926926-94-0 (ebook)

Published by:

In Our Words Inc.

Distributed by:

Instagram & Twitter: @bstellargroup
E-Mail: info@bstellargroup
Website: bstellargroup.com
Telephone: 416-214-6899

Dedication

I dedicate this book to my mother
— Winnifred Berry —
Her love for me is matchless and unconditional.
I am thankful for the life lessons she taught me,
and will uphold the values she instilled in me.

Table of Contents

Prologue ~ Stacey Ann Berry.................................... 1
Hidden Secrets 12
I Shall... 13
How Can my Existence be Denied?....................... 14
Adam's Weaker Vessel 15
Warriors in God's Kingdom.................................... 16
Through a Dolphin's Eyes 20
Inside Religion 21
Life Got Better to Get Worse................................. 22
Love Thy Enemy as Myself..................................... 23
Keep Shining Your Light 26
Rise Above Life's Storms.. 27
Real Motivation 28
Resilience.. 29
Never Let This World Steal Your Joy 30
Journey to Peace 31
Living Your True Purpose...................................... 32
A Godlike Frame of Mind...................................... 36
Soul Searching... 37
What is the Soul?... 38
My Inner Spirit.. 39
Intimacy with God 40
God's Garden... 44
Make a Vow... 45
Always Remain 46
My Heart Smiles 50
God's Grace 51
In the Life After 54
One Sweet Day 55
A Special Dedication to My Mother....................... 57

Winnie, a Golden Heart *59*
Only a Mother *60*
True Meaning of Retirement *61*
My Mother's Words of Wisdom *63*
My Mom's Favourite Quotes *65*
My Mother's Notes of Encouragement *69*
The Life & Legacy of Winnifred Berry *99*
September 23, 1940 - July 25, 2016 .... *99*
Endorsements *105*
About the Author *108*

Prologue ~ Stacey Ann Berry

Deeper Reflections of Life:
Words to inspire the heart and uplift the soul

I wrote my first poem at the age of 17, which I read at my cousin's funeral. He lost his life to gun violence when he was 22. Almost a year later, I wrote a poem called "In Life After" as a tribute to my maternal grandmother, Estella McKenzie, who passed away from a heart attack the day after my birthday on May 4, 1999. I then gave copies of this poem as a gift to people who had lost a loved one. I began to get requests to write personalized poems for funerals, birthdays and special occasions.

I wrote a poem called "The True Meaning of Retirement" and gave it to each guest at my mom's surprise retirement party which I had the honour of organizing. I also started writing love songs and gospel songs at the age of 19. I wrote most of my poems on the train as I traveled to York University. I enjoyed writing poetry because I wanted to uplift and comfort those who had lost a loved one. It also became a constructive way to express my pain and frustration.

As I reflect on my journey as a writer, I never knew that my pain would give me purpose and the tragic loss of my cousin would lead me to create poems that comfort and inspire others.

I never imagined in my wildest dreams that I would be an author. As a child I was always fascinated with books. I spent countless hours alone in my room reading or making images more vibrant in my colouring books. Every time my parents took me out, I never left home without a book. It was like my purse before I was old enough to have one, or my cell phone that today I never leave home without. As early as elementary school, writing a story was my most enjoyable assignment in school. I would get lost in coming up with names for my characters, developing the plot and making characters out of construction paper who looked like me, my friends or my family.

Reading was my way to escape into another world of adventure and it kept me focused. It inspired me to believe anything was possible. Surprisingly, reading and writing was something I struggled with. I could not understand why as a studious and hardworking student, my grades were so low.

In grade three, I was diagnosed with a learning disability and placed in special education classes until grade six. The entire experience caused my self-esteem and confidence to plummet. Many of my classmates made cruel comments and laughed at me for being a slow learner. I would keep working hard, but could never earn high grades. By the time I got to high school, there was some improvement with my grades. I had high grade in some classes, but a C in most. I did not enjoy high school, but I loved learning. I would usually pass on hanging out with my friends during lunch and hang out at the library instead. I dreamt of becoming a lawyer and knew I had to work extra hard, especially since I was not an A student. When I got into college, my grades began to skyrocket. I completed my first year at Ryerson University with all A's. All of my hard work paid off.

In spite of having a difficult time in school, I was blessed with a phenomenal mother and an amazing sister who were invested in my academic success. They inspired me to love education and learning. They helped shape who I am today and influenced my journey to success.

My sister, Christine Ittai, gave me books written by authors like Judy Blume, and books about freedom fighters like the autobiography of Malcolm X. I loved reading stories of how African-Americans overcame hardships, discrimination and excelled against all odds. Of all the books she gave me, *I Know Why The Caged Bird Sings,* by Maya Angelou, became my absolute favourite. That was when I discovered how to use words in a new way. I discovered the power of poetry and how this art form can comfort the soul, enlighten the mind and soothe a broken heart. My sister had a profound impact on my learning. My fondest memories are of asking her, "What does this word mean?" In a stern but loving, gentle voice, her response was always the same: "Look it up in a dictionary, write it down, and memorize it." She would tell me to make a new vocabulary word list every summer. We would review it and she would test me on the spelling and meaning of each word.

In addition to my word list, as I got older, I began to fill notebooks with lyrics of songs I heard on the radio from my favourite R&B artists. I would keep a list of quotes I read in *Ebony* and *Essence* Magazines. I was always motivated by positive words and phrases by African-American civil rights leaders, entrepreneurs, authors and influencers. As I look back this was all preparing me for my journey as a writer, author, songwriter, influencer and entrepreneur.

Of all the knowledge I gained from books and formal education, nothing compares to the lessons and values I received from my beloved mother, Winnifred Berry.

My mother gave me my first children's Bible which I still have today. She ensured our home was filled with books, poems, positive affirmations and unconditional love.

When I was diagnosed with a learning disability, she intervened by tutoring me at home. When a subject was beyond her ability to teach, she sent me to English and math tutors. She enrolled me in piano lessons to give me the opportunity to explore my musical skills. She knew, before I did, that I was gifted musically, and she called me her singing bird. When I began to write poetry, speeches and songs, she was my first audience and biggest fan. She was the first person to purchase my poems "In The Life After" and "One Sweet Day" to give them as gifts to her friends who had lost loved ones.

Although my self-confidence was low, my mom made me feel like I was capable of anything! Every time I complained about reaching my goals, she would say, "If yuh waan good yuh nose haffi run," which means if you want to go far in life, you have to work hard. Every time I felt like dropping out of school, she would say, "A quitter never wins and a winner never quits."

When I was accepted to college my mom rejoiced. When I graduated from college, she came to my graduation with a heart full of joy and pride. When I graduated with my first degree from York University, she held a surprise graduation party. When I got my master's degree, she knew I was on my way to build a future brighter than she had imagined. What I always appreciated about my mom is that she did not make me feel like her love was conditional upon my success in school. She wanted me to know that whatever path I chose to pursue, she expected me to give it my best shot. She did not pressure me to get all A's, but she wanted me to value having higher education and understand the power of being able to stand on my own feet.

I developed my work ethic from my mother who worked as a nurse for 27 years. She usually worked 12-hour shifts, and occasionally 19 hours, and sometimes 24 hours. When I saw her working this hard, my dream was to earn enough money to help her retire early so she could travel, put her feet up and relax. When she told me her life story of how she immigrated to Canada from Jamaica through the "West Indian Domestic Scheme" and the low wages she was paid, it broke my heart. It was shocking to learn that my mother lived in a country where she earned a significantly lower wage and did not have equal opportunities because she was an immigrant, a woman and a person of African-Caribbean heritage.

From a young age, I became very aware of what racism and hate felt like. This awareness led to my love for books about the Civil Rights Movement, the teachings of Martin Luther King and Marcus Garvey, and W. E. B. Dubois, which taught me to see strength in hardship and beauty in struggle. It also sparked frustration with injustice, oppression and racism that was buried deep within the legal system. Nonetheless, I felt very hopeful about my ability to be successful. I developed a strong sense of pride in my African-Caribbean culture, became motivated by the positive contributions made by my race and felt deeply connected to my heritage. As a child I had a lovely cultural mix of friends and still maintain this diversity in my friendships today.

Life growing up was not peaches and roses. I attended high school in a neighbourhood plagued by crime and violence. Yet, my mom taught me I did not have to be a product of my environment or accept the negative labels thrown at me. Both of my parents, especially my dad, taught me to be a leader and not a follower. I grew up in a strict household where I was expected to use my spare time wisely. This gave me the discipline to be focused and complete high school, but my GPA was not high enough to attend University right out of the gate. I decided to attend college in order to prepare for University. After a few failed attempts, I finally got accepted into York University in 2004.

Although my experience is not unique, my prospects would have been very different if it had not been for the dedication, love and support of my parents, and especially my mother. Having a parent who stayed up with me late at night to review research papers helped me move to the next level, year after year.

My mother went above and beyond to help me with my learning: She also became a tutor and cheerleader for hundreds of other children. She began tutoring me at home when I was in grade three. About a year later, she started a Saturday class in the basement of our family home. She would tutor my cousins, the children of neighbours and friends. She eventually decided to register a tutoring business called Back to Basics Learning Centre, which turned our home into a community centre for parents in need of advice and students who had been diagnosed with learning disabilities.

My mom believed every child was capable of learning. The motto for her company was, "Every child is a winner."

She conducted research on early childhood development. She purchased hundreds of books from Jamaica and created a curriculum that met the mandate of the Ministry of Education in Ontario. Her method of teaching was influenced by the education she received at Keith Basic School in Jamaica. She believed that many children were not doing well in school because the Canadian school system did not emphasize the basic foundations of literacy prior to kindergarten. She did not agree a hundred percent with Jean Piaget's development theory, which is based on the notion that children learn through play. My mom believed that play was natural for children. She felt the Canadian school system should include rote learning or memorization techniques and a phonetic method of teaching children, especially during pre-school. She believed rote learning with a combination of Jean Piaget's development theory would help students who had learning disabilities better grasp fundamentals of math, science, grammar and the rules of writing. She also felt that the school system should incorporate all of the key learning styles in the classroom such as visual, audio and kinesthetic. She used music and dance to make learning fun! She was on a mission to help children who were diagnosed with learning disabilities and behavioural challenges. Her dream was to have her method of teaching integrated into the Canadian school system.

My mom was a serious multitasker. In addition to being a registered practical nurse, she was a registered babysitter. Our family home was filled with children of various cultural backgrounds and ethnicities. She also had exceptional culinary skills. She made the best cakes, muffins and a wide variety of Jamaican dishes. People would drop by our home just to eat. While she worked nights as a nurse at Toronto General Hospital, she ran her tutoring business on Saturdays and after school. After she retired from nursing, she ran her tutoring classes full time six days a week from 8:00 am to 6:00 pm.

My mom, affectionately known as Mrs. Berry, was like a

mother to many of her clients, a second mom to her students and an advocate for learning. She would visit youth in prison, attend parent-teacher meetings and write letters to appeal suspensions. Mrs. Berry began each day in her classroom with *The Child's Prayer* and the song *This Little Light of Mine*. My dad's friend built her a classroom at the back of the family home. Ninety percent of the advertising for her tutoring services was done by referrals. Mrs. Berry provided meals, prayed with her students and made them fall in love with learning. Many of her students received scholarships, graduated with honours and pursued graduate or professional degrees. The majority of these students were falling through the cracks of the public school system had low self-esteem. It was rare to go out into the community and not run into a parent or student who did not know Mrs. Berry.

My sweet and precious mother passed away on July 25, 2016 from colon cancer, 10 months after her 75th birthday. I hoped and prayed for her to live a longer life. I asked God, why did He take her so soon, and so quickly? Why did such a phenomenal, loving, forgiving, caring woman have to die of such a terrible, merciless and aggressive disease? Being told she had rare form of cancer that would get worse rapidly was like walking through the valley of death. I was so angry. I prayed, screamed and yelled. I begged God to give my mom a second chance to live. All of the prayers from those who loved her went unanswered. This made me more furious. It shook my faith and my reason for living to the core. Witnessing my mother slowly wither away and end up on life support felt like a part of me was dying with her.

My mom was the strongest and most amazing person I knew. She was the one that her friends and family went to when they were sick or needed advice, a good meal, or prayer. To see her lose her strength and ability to do all the things she loved, such as cook, teach and entertain friends and family, was devastating. Each doctor's visit to North York General Hospital, sitting with her and watching her body being injected with that poisonous chemotherapy treatment, was traumatic beyond comprehension. Getting the news from the doctor that the treatment was no longer working as she lay in the hospital was the most helpless I have ever felt in my life.

The one thing my mom did not lose was her faith in God and her ability to pray. While she was severally sick with barely any strength to move, she continued to pray for others. She continued to give advice to anyone who called her for help. She continued to laugh with such joy that you would never know she was seriously ill by the sound of her voice. She never lost hope and still imparted words of encouragement when I was frustrated and angry at the thought of losing her. She still found the strength to drive herself to the store to buy my last birthday card two months before she passed away.

The loss of my mother was devastating. She was not just a great mother who had given birth to me, but she was my best friend, cheerleader and prayer warrior. It is a pain that never goes away. It feels like a deep part of me is gone forever. The joys of the holidays and family gatherings died with her. People who I thought were family went ghost. I am not sure how long it will take for me to heal and if I ever will, but I have comfort in knowing I can turn to God when my faith gets weak, when my patience runs thin or when I am crippled by fear.

My mom's last advice to me before she lost her ability to speak was, "Trust God." The most precious gift that my mom gave me was her faith in God. She did not just tell me about the love of God, she showed it to me through her actions, unconditional love, support and compassion every single day of her life. She left behind a wonderful legacy and made a positive impact on the lives of so many people. She meant the world to so many of her students, family and friends. She left me with her friends who are like aunties to me, whom I am still very close to today. They helped me get through the toughest time in my life. These phenomenal women remained by her side during her illness and expressed how much they loved her. She would always say, "Good friends are better than pocket money." Her friends are sure worth more than all the riches in the world.

My mom will always be God's greatest blessing to me. I always told her there is not enough money in the world to repay her for all of her love and sacrifice. My entire emotional, psychological, intellectual and spiritual development was influenced by my mother. She was my biggest cheerleader and supporter. I owe my success to her.

Now that she is gone, I know that no one will love or care for me as much as she did. It gives me so much peace to know that she knew how much I loved and cherished her. We spent so much one-on-one time together she would ask me if I was tired of hanging out with her. When I told her I loved her, she would say, "I know, Stacey."

Deeper Reflections of Life is a tribute to my mom, Winnifred Berry. It is a celebration of her life and legacy. The poems in this book are inspired by the Christian faith and my spiritual journey in developing a deeper understanding of God. There is also a chapter titled, "My Mother's Words of Wisdom," which includes her favourite quotes and words of encouragement that she wrote in my birthday and Christmas cards over the years.

My mom heard almost every poem in this book, including the ones I wrote about her. She used to tell me that I need to publish my poems. I told her that when I do, my book will be titled *Deeper Reflections of Life*. She gave me her stamp of approval.

Awaken Your Mind

"Truth crushed to earth shall rise again."
~ *William Cullen Bryant*

Hidden Secrets

In the beginning God made the heavens and the earth
Since the half of the story has been told
the TRUTH is hard to behold
Although I am told it is wrong to LIE,
it is like this world has got my mind hypnotized
with illusions and false delusions
HIS or HERSTORY is hidden
and rewritten to cause confusion
I just rely on God's light to help me
decide how to win spiritual fights
Sometimes my soul cries at night
Every time I walk through the valley
of the shadow of death,
God is my bulletproof vest
My quest is to see the depths of a person's soul,
right through their eyes because
that is where HIDDEN SECRETS hide,
but it is hard to see the TRUTH if
LIES keep being told
It is only through the LIGHT of Christ
the HIDDEN SECRETS unfold

I Shall

I SHALL walk amongst those who are like wolves in sheep's clothing
I SHALL walk in the pathway of those who do not want to see me achieve
I SHALL shine my light into those living in darkness without engaging in physical fights
I SHALL rise against depression and strife
I SHALL not sit in the seat of the scornful, but speak uplifting words while in the presence of the mournful
I SHALL observe my surroundings so that I can make wise moves, since life is like a game of chess
I SHALL not waste my precious time in empty conversations like a spider in a web of mess
I SHALL not allow my thoughts to feed on lust, which leads to jealously, impurity and relationships without security
I SHALL walk through the fire and not get burned for becoming one with God is my only concern

How Can my Existence be Denied?

If you believe in love and I AM love,
    how can my existence be denied?
If you desire peace and I AM peace,
    how can my existence be denied?
If you want happiness and I AM joy,
    how can my existence be denied?
If you want honesty and I AM truth,
    how can my existence be denied?
If you believe in knowledge and I AM wisdom,
    how can my existence be denied?
If you desire courage and I AM strength,
    how can my existence be denied?
If you ask for grace and I give you mercy,
    how can my existence be denied?
If you want to live and I AM the giver of life,
    how can my existence be denied?

Adam's Weaker Vessel

Where is the safe haven for Adam's weaker vessel?
Adam's weaker vessel was blamed for turning the Garden of Eden into an unhappy home
How could a weaker vessel teach Adam to stand tall after his fall?
Where is the story about the day when Eve chose to snatch her soul back from the Devil, who wants to see God's children stray, or did that half of the story just fade away?

Women reclaimed their position in the Kingdom of God in the story of Deborah, a leader who resolved disputes and motivated her followers
Women demonstrated the importance of loyalty in the story of Ruth who remained devoted to her mentor Naomi
God gave women courage to be advocates like Esther
God gave women faith to believe in miracles the way Mary of Nazareth did
God created women to be by men's side and gave them strength to withstand challenges and hardships, as demonstrated by Coretta Scott-King during the Civil Rights Movement
When a man reclaims his position in the Kingdom of God, he will realize that the woman he chooses to marry is not his weaker vessel, but is his pillar of strength

Warriors in God's Kingdom

Warriors in God's kingdom are armed with scripture for every battle
Warriors in God's kingdom surround themselves with people who care about their well-being
Warriors in God's kingdom are quick to forgive, pray every night and day
Warriors in God's kingdom refuse to compromise their values, remain true to their purpose and calling
Warriors in God's kingdom conquer fear with faith and are not afraid of failure
They bounce back with no regrets
Warriors in God's kingdom plant seeds of love and joy in the heart of everyone they meet
Warriors in God's kingdom believe in time they will reap what they sow
When faced with sadness and disappointment, God's warriors reminisce on moments of inspiration
God's warriors remain on the right side of history or herstory
God's warriors demand justice, fight for freedom and make peace with their enemies
God's warriors have endless hope, for they know that the Lord already won battle for their soul

Heartbreaking Reality

"Because lawlessness is increased,
most people's love will grow cold."
~ Matthew 24:12

Through a Dolphin's Eyes

When I swim around my home, I cannot help but notice how filthy it has become
When I look to my right, I see the leftovers from the food that humans eat
When I look to my left, I see paper and hundreds of metal cans thrown into my home by careless human hands
When I look at the bottom of the sea, I see garbage everywhere!
When I swim above the waters, I see plastic bottles and crude oil floating around without any concern for my environment
Don't these humans realize that my entire family lives here? How I wish for my home to be as clean as the day when my ancestors first arrived
No matter how many wishes I make, more garbage shows up as the days pass by
I can no longer find food that is free from pollutants and disease
The toxins from all this junk are spreading to my unborn seed
Each day it is getting harder for me to breathe and too cloudy for me to see
Lately, I have a more urgent wish to make
I am worried that my species will become extinct sooner than most people think
Those who admire my beauty will no longer hear my laughter, marvel at my intelligence or enjoy acrobatic tricks
One day, I might only exist in books, photographs and movies.
Many will wonder if my entire species was only a myth…

Inside Religion

The collection plate is passed around every week
    sometimes used to oppress the poor, while through taxes
    the government takes more and more
Would I call the police if Christ came to my house like a thief
    in the night through my back door?
INSIDE RELIGION, many are called, but so many more are
    here to confuse the chosen few
INSIDE RELIGION, many will come in the name of the
    Lord, but believe them not
It is sad to say, but some of them only want the money you
    got
Stealing all in the name of the Lord, as they selfishly enjoy
    their wealth,
While millions of people from around the globe suffer from
    oppression, human trafficking, starvation and poor health
God made mankind, but mankind manipulated "scriptural
    teachings" to divide races and misguide true believers
At the same time ignoring the voice of the innocent in prison

INSIDE RELIGION, the preacher's wife can be abused and
    battered, while her husband climbs up the economic
    ladder
INSIDE RELIGION, some hide behind "good deeds" but
    lack love, peace, mercy and compassion
INSIDE RELIGION, there are hypocrisies and false
    teachings
Inside God is TRUTH, PEACE, GRACE, LOVE and
    FORGIVENESS
Once you develop a personal relationship with God, you
    will be able to discern when pastors mislead their
    congregation, and exploit the gospel
Inside God, the truth of Christ is revealed; you will find the
    Kingdom of Heaven and not be deceived
The life of Christ is a miraculous story that I choose to believe

Life Got Better to Get Worse

Today it may seem like we live in a better society
But we have been deceived to believe that it is normal to regulate a person's every move
We have given up part of our freedom to invade each other's privacy
With the rise of reality T.V., social media and the "selfie" culture, we've demolished the meaning of a private and sacred lifestyle
The media has gotten its viewers so comfortable in monitoring people's lives
That we don't bother to question why there is a camera on every street corner
We don't bother to question why technology has us hypnotized
Our society has become worse than spies
No one bothers to question why technology has become our master
Once we are offered 'digital currency' many of us will take it without hesitation
Most people will submit to the ideologies of a cashless society
Many people will become so dependent on credit and debit that it will become the only legal way to obtain the basic necessities of life
Once everyone's heart is filled with fear, the day is near when liberty is completely forsaken
Freedom will become irrelevant and deemed a forbidden reality
It will be too late when we realize that we gave away the gift of freedom
It will be too late when we realize that we gave up our constitutional right to privacy
It will be too late when we realize that we are living like prisoners without bars
It will be too late when we realize that we paid a huge price to become slaves to technology

Love Thy Enemy as Myself

How do I love my enemies as myself?
How do I love someone who stabs me in the back after I have
    been a loyal friend?
If he showed me violence once, he will show it twice
How can I bless those who hate to see me live?
How can I be kind to those who exploit my skills and talents?
I was taught to conquer my enemies by trusting in Christ
God's son loves us so much He gave His life
Not just for my sins alone, but my foes
Everyone deserves salvation and yearns for restoration
I am thankful to God for preparing a table of my blessings in
    the presence of my enemies
The more I give God glory, the more I will find the strength
    to love my enemies as myself
As difficult as this may seem, I pray for the courage to show
    love to my enemies.
In spite of what others say, it's God's way

Never Give Up!

"Most of the important things in this world have been accomplished by people who have kept on trying when there seemed to be no hope at all."

~ **Dale Carnegie**

Keep Shining Your Light

When you feel like your strength is wearing thin
Stay hopeful and depend on your faith within
Allow patience and love to be your guard
These are the jewels you will need when life gets hard
Keep shining your light through life's strains
Sometimes it has to rain
To wash away the pain
After moments of sorrow
The sun will shine tomorrow
Sometimes you have to fall
To learn how to stand strong and tall
You may not achieve everything your heart desires
But you can strive to live by the principles you admire
Don't waste time or run through life too fast
Savour each moment because you never know which day will be your last
During the darkest moments in your life
Keep shining your light because that is when it is most bright

Rise Above Life's Storms

To rise above life's storms, you need the kind of peace that surpasses all understanding
In the midst of heartache and pain, an ounce of compassion will help you rise again
When life fails to meet your expectations, become a beacon of hope to others and you will find restoration
When you feel like life is overwhelming, use your inner strength to rise above difficult circumstances
When the waves of life knock you down, have confidence in knowing that God's strength will help you rebound
Refuse to live in doubt and fear; believe that you will not encounter more challenges than you can bear
Be confident about your talents and spiritual gifts
Pray continuously
Have faith that miracles still happen unexpectedly
When nothing seems to be going right, life's storms should not cause you to lose sleep at night
Challenges shape our character, test our faith and make us wiser
Be thankful for the rough waves of life and enjoy the ride with a smile
No matter how hard life seems, you will rise above life's storms and achieve your dreams

Real Motivation

Real motivation requires you to pick a goal and stick to it, no matter the number of obstacles in your way
Real motivation is going the extra mile, no matter the length of the task
Real motivation is finding a way to be optimistic
Real motivation means you will see the good in others and not allow pessimism to cloud your judgment
Real motivation is taking a leap of faith even when you do not see the whole staircase
Real motivation means to be confident, courageous and strong
You will take bold steps when others say you're wrong

Resilience

Resilience does not get crushed by rejection, and keeps trying
  over and over again
Resilience bounces back after facing failure
Resilience knocks on doors until one opens
Resilience relies on patience to get the right opportunity
Resilience will never surrender until it finds a pot of gold and
  knows goals never grow old
Resilience is how Thomas Edison invented the light bulb
Resilience remains best friends with courage and persistence
Resilience knows that faith and hard work turns dreams into
  reality

Never Let This World Steal Your Joy

There are so my ways this world will try to steal your joy,
    whether it is a job loss, failed relationship, sickness or the
    death of a loved one
These unfortunate situations will make you feel like the
    ground from beneath you vanished
When you are running on empty, connect to the joy of the
Lord for strength
When you cannot find a reason to smile, sing an inspirational
song or dance freely in your own style
Joy is not like happiness which depends on good things
    happening
Joy can be felt when you are not defined by your wealth or
    accolades
Joy can be felt each time you count your blessings
Joy can be felt when bad things work in your favour
Joy can be felt when you focus on the solutions to your
    problems
Joy can be felt when your faith feels bigger than your fears
Joy can be felt in the midst of sorrow, pain and tears
Joy can be felt after you lose all you gained,
    because the sun always comes out after the rain

Journey to Peace

The road to peace is narrow and long
On this road you will not find any glitz or glamour
Peace does not exist in war or conflict
Peace does not exist in envy, jealously, anger or hate
Peace does not exist in malice or revenge
Peace does not exist in avarice or greed
Peace thrives when you accept that love is all you need
Peace can be felt when the beauty of nature makes your heart smile
Peace can be felt when you take the time to slow down, reflect and smell the roses
Peace can be felt when you are content knowing your time on earth is well spent
Peace can be felt when you accept yourself and believe you are enough
Peace can be felt when you appreciate your ability to make a dollar out of 15 cents
Peace can be felt when you are grateful for the little things and gifts from the heart
When you fill your soul with peace, every day feels like a new start

Living Your True Purpose

Be in tune with your gifts and talents
Assess your likes and dislikes
Refuse to compromise your faith and values for success
Stand by your principles
Be authentic and live with integrity
Pay attention to opportunities that choose you
Do what makes you happy while ensuring God is pleased
Visualize yourself where you want to be
Speak positively of others and yourself
Identify what you would do with your time if you had all the
    money in the world
Live as though it were your last day
Never be afraid to let others know
    when you are not doing okay
Take a leap of faith and pursue your dreams
Say yes to the right opportunities
Living your true purpose takes time to discover, but if you are
    connected to your inner spirit, it will be revealed

My Soul Says Yes!

"He restoreth my soul:
He leadeth me in the paths of righteousness
for His name's sake."

~ Palms 23:3 KJV

A Godlike Frame of Mind

Lord, recreate the way I think so that I can conquer any
 obstacle that comes my way
Give me a mind that meditates on Your Holy Word and
 things pure and divine
Train my mind to decipher the signs of the enemy's tricks
So that I don't get misled by wolves in sheep's clothing
Teach me how to maintain a positive frame of mind in the
 midst of my adversities
A Godlike frame of mind does not feed on lust or yearn for
 things unjust
A Godlike frame of mind turns war into peace
Knows that it is wiser to feed your enemies with compassion,
 forgiveness and kindness, rather than vengeance,
 and a cold heart
As a child of God, I was born to win
I cannot allow my mind to become contaminated by this
 world filled with sin
Many people have a damaged frame of mind filled with
 regrets, pain and sorrow
If I let God be at the centre of it all, I will stop trying to be in
 control and have less stress
I pray to have a mind like the Son of God, Jesus Christ
So that I will continuously praise God with all my might
 and meditate on his wonder-working power day and night

Soul Searching

My soul is searching to connect with the Most High God,
   Jehovah, giver of life
My soul wants to become in sync with the spirit of God who
   put the clouds in the sky
My mind wants to lead my every move, but my eyes
   determine my thoughts, while my heart says let go and let
   God decide how I speak or teach and where I walk
If I do not use the Holy Spirit more than my flesh, I will wind
   up feeling stressed and depressed
My soul is searching to connect with a higher power who will
   prevent me from falling, but adores me and understands
   my core being
Whenever Christ knocks, I will quickly grab His hand

What is the Soul?

What is the soul when a child is born?
Is it already fully grown or does it age as we age?
Is it that guiding force for the blind?
Can it still hear if a child is born deaf?
Is it what brings us closer to God when we feel like we have nothing left?
Maybe it is that fighting force that causes us to never give up after we have tried our best
When our body gets sick, does it feel pain or does it help us to stand through life's strains?
What does the soul do when a woman is told she has only three days to live?
Does it give her chance to see day four or more?
What does a soul do when the seed of life is planted inside a woman's womb, but does not bear fruit?
What happens to the soul when a young child is violated of their purity?
Does it run and hide or forever cry inside?
What does a soul do when it sees its body searching for love in all the wrong places and constantly deceived?
Does the soul find true love that our eyes cannot see?
When the soul sees its body struggling to survive, can it shape our destiny or is that up to the Most High?
Once we are buried six feet deep, does the soul enter into another human being, creatures or remain unseen?
As we lay in eternal sleep, does the soul return to heaven when it knows we're okay?
Or remain on earth until judgment day?

My Inner Spirit

My inner spirit is not the reflection in the mirror
It does not keep recollections of wrongs or sorrows
Nor does it worry about tomorrow
It is not my gender, age or race
But allows me to choose to live in misery or grace
My inner spirit is placed inside my body by God, not some
 mystic Darwinian ideology
My inner spirit cannot feel the cut of a knife, but it helps me
 to prevail against oppression and strife
It knows me better than I know myself
It can see the ills of the world through a child's eyes
It's that miraculous breath of life that keeps me alive
It's life's invisible wonders
It's what makes me reflect and ponder
It's why caged birds sing
It's the unspeakable joy within
It's the talents I bring
It's the light others see in my eyes
It's my spiritual battle between good and bad
It allows me to feel sad or glad
When I feed my inner spirit with God's word
It's filled with wisdom and power that guides me every
 second, minute and hour
It's what makes my heart smile, but it's only here for a short
 while

Intimacy with God

God I give you my heart, my soul and my body
I surrender my all to you
I cast all my burdens to you
I will no longer worry about what tomorrow will bring
I give all glory to you like the caged bird that sings
Help me to separate myself from all addictions and toxins
I need you to shower me with your Holy Spirit, love, grace and mercy
Recreate my wounded frame of mind
Teach me to meditate on things pure and divine
Take authority over principalities of darkness and those who block you from reaching me
Lord, I just want to be consecrated to you
So that you can order my steps in everything I do

Faith in God

"Our belief in God is not blind faith.
Belief is having a firm conviction something is true,
not hoping it's true."

~ Max Lucado

God's Garden

God is the vine and we are the branches
He is the root of all things pure and divine
Without Him we could not bear fruit
For He is the staff of life
Through Him we are able to grow and blossom into precious flowers
His Holy Word is sweeter than the first day of spring
It sends us energy more powerful than the sun on a hot summer day
His grace and mercy reminds us why it is so important to give thanks and pray
His anointing falls on us like *melodies from heaven* and rain from the sky
It washes away our sins and gives us the chance to find a new beginning
As long as we remain in God's Garden,
He will plant the seed of truth in our eyes
So that we can see through deception and lies
As long as we remain in God's Garden
He will plant the seed of faith in our feet
So that we can walk in His spirit and overcome defeat
As long as we remain in God's Garden
He will plant the seed of giving in our hands so that we can share our wealth with those whose cupboards are bare
As long as we remain in God's Garden
He will plant the seed of 'joy unspeakable' in our soul
So that we can praise Him while we are young and when we grow old
The most important seed that God will plant,
    as long as we give him a chance,
        is the seed of Christ in our heart so that we can have the strength to love and forgive others even when they tear our branches apart

Make a Vow

Make a vow to Forgiveness
And your heart will not be filled with resentment
Make a vow to Honesty
And you will speak words of sincerity
Make a vow to unselfish ambition
And you will be driven to serve humanity
Make a vow to live by God's Spirit
And you will not be controlled by the evil desires of your flesh
Make a vow to stand up for your beliefs
And you will not hesitate to do what is right
Make a vow to hold onto Peace
And take it with you everywhere you go
Make a vow to Faith
And like a mustard seed, it will grow
Make a vow to Love
And like the moon in the dark night, your beauty will glow

Always Remain

ALWAYS REMAIN **Thankful** for the gift of life, freedom and good health
Be careful not to trade any of these precious jewels for wealth
ALWAYS REMAIN **Obedient** to God's Wisdom
And you will not continue to repeat the same mistakes
ALWAYS REMAIN **Loyal** to Family and Friends,
by helping them fight the battles that life sends
ALWAYS REMAIN **Merciful** to your foes
Instead of showing vengeance for their woes
ALWAYS REMAIN **Strong**
Especially when everything in your life seems to go wrong
ALWAYS REMAIN **Humble**
And do not lose composure when you stumble
ALWAYS REMAIN on the pathway of **Honesty**
Instead of convincing yourself to believe
that the pathway of lies is an easier route
ALWAYS REMAIN **Confident** about doing what is right
And never give in to the voice of doubt
ALWAYS REMAIN **True** to yourself
Instead of being a replica of someone else
ALWAYS REMAIN **Brave**
by using the **Courage** that God gave
And do not allow fear to stop you
from achieving the goals you choose
You have nothing to lose
But so much to gain if you ALWAYS REMAIN
Grateful, Forgiving, Kind & True
It is only through these virtues,
that you can fulfill the main reason for your existence,
which is to spread God's **Love**
that resides deep inside of you

Fill My Heart with Compassion

"If you want others to be happy, practice compassion.
If you want to be happy, practice compassion."

~ Dalai Lama

My Heart Smiles

When I see my mother enjoy a cup of tea, while we spend quality time, my heart smiles

When I watch my father dance to reggae music I have not heard in a long while, my heart smiles

When I speak to my sister and she offers me words of hope and wisdom, my heart smiles

When I see my nephews striving to make their dreams reality, my heart smiles

When I meet up with friends for lunch or dinner, my heart smiles

When I reminisce on the adventurous, fun, and magical times I experienced as a child, my heart smiles

When life becomes too hard to bear and I hear God say, "It will get better," my heart smiles

When I think about how much God loves me, my heart smiles

God's Grace

Makes me blind to our differences
GOD'S GRACE
Heals pain and prevents hate
GOD'S GRACE
Fills me up with love and peace
GOD'S GRACE
Allows me to forgive those who hate to see me live
GOD'S GRACE
Keeps me smiling when the sun is not shining
GOD'S GRACE
Helps me to feel another person's pain after losing all the wealth I gained
GOD'S GRACE
Anoints me with unspeakable joy and glory
GOD'S GRACE
Lifts my spirit up after a tragic lesson
GOD'S GRACE
Enlightens my mind so that I can find the true meaning of heaven
God gave me GRACE so that I can shine my light in the darkest place brighter than the moonlight in the sky
God's GRACE is a gift that I am blessed to receive
It is so powerful it can cure any disease, heal broken hearts and mend deep scars
God's GRACE has been there for me to find, but first I had to leave the ills of my past behind

Eternal Life

"For our light and momentary troubles
are achieving for us an eternal glory
that far outweighs them all.
So we fix our eyes not on what is seen,
but on what is unseen,
since what is seen is temporary,
but what is unseen is eternal."

~ 2 Corinthians 4:17-18

In the Life After

We sometimes wonder
Where our loved ones might be
They reside nearby
In places that our eyes cannot see
In our dreams they show us signs
To guide us in this life of good and bad times
Every time it rains, God showers us with their love
While they continue to watch over us
From the heavens in the sky above
Like immortal angels they stand
Their spirit is always there to hold our hand
Deep inside our heart they will always remain
If we listen closely
We can still hear them say our name
As we enjoy life, they are patiently waiting
With open arms and soft laughter
To greet us in the life after

Dedicated to my late grandmother Estella McKenzie - June 12, 1912 to May 4, 1999

One Sweet Day

When we lose the ones closest to our hearts
We wish they never had to depart
Eventually we will realize
They must one day pass away
To a life filled with better and brighter days
Their departure from earth is their first step towards
Living in the spirit
So that they may have the opportunity
To have complete unity
With God and His Angels until eternity
No longer are they in bondage to the flesh
No longer do they have to live
In pain, misery and distress
For the first time
Sight is given to those who used to be blind
Those who were once deaf in this life
Now have the ability to hear
Our cries when we shed tears
Listen to our voices when we talk
And our steps as we walk
Although it is hard to ignore the pain we feel today,
Just remember, after our time on earth is complete,
Each of us will have the chance to greet our loved ones,
Who left us behind one sweet day

Dedicated to those who lost their battle to cancer

A Special Dedication to My Mother

"Give me flowers while I am living." ~ Unknown

My mother always said, "Give me flowers while I am living." I cherished her as often as possible and spent quality time until she asked "Stacey, aren't you tired of seeing me?" My response was, "Mom, I need you in reserve."

We had such a special bond and were inseparable, even until the day she passed away. I promised her that I would be by her side. I am thankful to God I was able to be there for her when she needed me most. It was through her sickness that I learned what love and true friendship looked like.

Winnie, a Golden Heart

Wisdom shared from a deep place of compassion and understanding

Investments made in the academic development of youth and children

Nurtures family and friends with unconditional love and hospitality

Never ceases praying to transform dreams into reality

Inspires others to be forgiving and as harmless as a flower

Encourages her children to have faith in the Higher Power

*A birthday tribute for my mom's 75 birthday gala,
September 23, 2015*

Only a Mother

Only a mother's **heart** is so tender that she embraces unconditional love

Only a mother **magnifies,** the virtuous woman described in **Proverbs 31:** "She is clothed with strength and dignity, she can laugh at the days to come. She speaks with wisdom and faithful instruction is on her tongue"

Only the **words** of a mother are so powerful that they can provide comfort to a hurting child

Only the **voice** of a mother is so soothing, it can dry the tears of a child's cry

Only the **eyes** of a mother can see the pain behind a child's smile

Only the **hands** of a mother are willing to give her children her last dime, or last slice of bread

Only the **feet** of a mother would walk a thousand miles just to gather food for her children

Only the **prayers** of a mother can comfort a child with a broken soul

Only a mother is **patient** enough to still have faith in a child who has been labeled 'out of control'

Only a mother would not hesitate to take the clothes off her back to **protect** a child from the cold

Only a mother would eagerly sell everything she has just to pay the rent

Only a mother's **instinct** can detect sickness in a child before he or she utters a word

A mother's **love** is everlasting, consistent, limitless, unselfish and sincere

When no one else cares, our mother is always there

This is why we must cherish and appreciate our mothers every second of the day

Not only because of the sacrifices she makes, but because a mother is someone who can never be replaced.

True Meaning of Retirement

Rise out of the workforce completely for eternity
Enjoy life's wonders abundantly
Time to reconnect with family and friends
Inspire others with your talents and smiles
Remember the days you spent as a child
Encourage others to keep striving to success
Make it a reality for all your dreams to be achieved
Evolve and blossom
Never forget you were born to win
Time to travel to all the beautiful places you have never been

My Mother's Words of Wisdom

In the last section of this book, I have included my Mom's favourite quotes and a collection of the notes she wrote to me in birthday and Christmas cards.

My Mom's Favourite Quotes

"Labour for learning before you grow old, for labour is better than silver and gold. Silver and gold will vanish away, but a good education will never decay."
~ *Desmond Dekker*

"The heights by great men reached and kept were not attained by sudden flight, but they, while their companions slept, were toiling upward in the night."
~ *Henry Wadsworth Longfellow*

"Winners never quit, and quitters never win."
~ *Vince Lombardi*

"Every mickle make a muckle, every muckle make a mickle."
~ *Jamaican proverb*

[Meaning—every small amount of effort or money gathered together will amount to something significant.]

"What don't cost life don't cost anything."
~ *Jamaican Proverb*

[Meaning—Your life is worth more than any material thing you can lose.]

"What is fi yuh can be unfiyuh." ~ **Jamaican Proverb**

[Meaning—If something belongs to you, no one else will get it.]

"Wha gone bad a maning, can't come good a evening."
 ~ **Jamaican Proverb**

[Meaning—When something goes wrong, do not spend time trying to fix it or dwell on it; let it go and move on.]

"If yuh wan good yuh nose haffi run."
 ~ ***Jamaican Proverb***

[Meaning—If you want to gain success, you have to work hard.]

"Good fren betta than packet money."
 ~ ***Jamaican Proverb***

[Meaning—Reliable and loyal friends are better than having cash or wealth.]

My Mother's Notes of Encouragement

My mother loved writing little notes of encouragement in cards. Here are some of my favourites.

Dec 05

STace honey
  If wishes were horses, all beggars would climb meaning our wish for you is that you have your hearts desire to the max. This is our gift for you. Will give you money for your printer in the week.

Have a
Merry Christmas
and a very
Happy New Year

Love you dearly
Mom & Dad

December 25, 2005

Stace honey,

If riches were horses, all the beggars would climb, meaning our wish for you is that you have your heart's desire to the max.

This is our gift for you. Will give you money for your printer this week.

> Love you dearly,
> Mom & Dad

14/9/05

Dearest Daughter,

Just want to say I did not forget I did not give you anything for your birthday but it's always better late than never. You light up my life you are my sunshine Although you can be moody at times but mom love for you never cease. Even when I am in Russia (smile) I will always be here for you. Keep up the good work. Always believe in yourself, search within your self and you will always find hope and strength for tomorrow.

Although this card may be too late for your birthday, it's never too late to wish you a year filled with happiness.
God bless you always.
With all my love.
mom.

September 14, 2005

A Belated Birthday Wish for You

Dearest Daughter,

Just want to say I did not forget. I did not give you anything for your birthday but it is always better late than never.

You light up my life. You are my sunshine.
Although you can be moody at times but Mom's love for you [will] never cease even when I am in Russia (smile). I will always be here for you.

Keep up the good work. Always believe in yourself. Search within yourself and you'll always find hope and strength for tomorrow.

God bless you always
With all my love,

Mom

3/5/06

Hi Stace,

I feel so blessed to have a beautiful child. I am just thanking god for you and pray he will give you health strength and happiness through out the years to come. and that he will keep me strong until you reach your goal and can be on your own. After that I am caput. Love you with all my heart soul and spirit. mom. gift later.

"O my wonderful daughter, thank God taht you live to see anoth-er day, may the good Lord keep and guide you in all that you are doing, and may the Lord order your steps in everything that you do, and protect you, happy birth day, from your dad
Sany B.

May 3, 2006

You Keep Getting Better Every Year

I feel so blessed to have a beautiful child.

I am just thanking God for you, and pray He will give you health, strength and happiness throughout the years to come, and that He will keep me strong until you reach your goal and be on your own. After that I can caput.

I love you with all my heart, soul and spirit,

Mom

Gift later.

Jan/06

Hi Stace

We may not have it to help you through school as we would like to; but we know you are very grateful for what you have or for what your dad and myself give you. You know we love you dearly and we will always be here for you. We wish you did not have to worry about how you are going to pay your school fee, but just focus on your studies. God provides for us and we will provide for you. Remember a quitter never wins, and a winner never quits. Love,

*I'm your friend,
I care
and I'm here for you
whenever
you need me.*

Stace darling you are special, you can make it to the top. Keep on keeping on. With God's guidance and my prayers for you, you shall overcome. Don't give up until you achieve your goal. Love you dearly, Mom

January 2006

Words of Encouragement

Hi Stace,

We may not have it to help you through school as I would like to but we know you are very grateful for what you have or for what your dad and myself give you. You know we love you dearly and we will always be here for you. We wish you did not have to worry about how you are going to pay for your school fees, but just focus on your studies. God provides for us and we will provide for you.

Remember a quitter never wins and a winner never quits.

Love.

Stace, darling you are special, you can make it to the top. Keep on keeping on. With God's guidance and my prayers for you, you shall overcome.

Don't give up until you achieve your goal.

Love you dearly,

Mom

May 3/07

Dearest Slace,

I thank my Heavenly Father for giving me such a beautiful daughter. I also thank Him for directing your steps and protecting you every step of your journey.

See life as a journey along the road. Some parts will be smooth, some will be rough and some in between; but all lead to a destination, and then you can rest and say thank God for a safe journey. I feel your pain as you pursue your career. I admire you for all you have done to accomplish your goal. You will finish money or not work or not. Our God is our provider. All the best. I love you dearly.

*Because you're special
in so many ways,
so warm, wonderful and dear.
These wishes for a perfect
and joyful day come with love
to last all through the year.

Happy Birthday!*

Mom.

May 3, 2007

Dearest Stace,

I thank my Heavenly Father for giving me such a beautiful daughter. I also thank Him for directing your steps and protecting you every step of your journey.

See life as a journey along the road. Some paths will be smooth. Some will be rough and some in between, but all lead to a destination and then you can rest and say thank God for a safe journey.

I feel your pain as you pursue your career. I admire you for all you have done to accomplish your goal. You will finish money or not, work or not. Our God is our Provider.

All the best, I love you dearly,

Mom

Note.
"Please find $26.00, one for each year. Plus what is in the first envelope and plus a treat on the weekend."

Love Mom

> May 3/08
>
> Dearest Stacey
>   I thank God for giving me such a lovely dthr. you are a blessing to the family. I wish I could make your dream come true by giving you your Lexus but you never know what God has in store but from you have Him Jason Dad your sis nephews aunts uncles

Each year we have another chance
To pause and start anew,
To add more meaning to our lives
And make our dreams come true...
And because a birthday is a sign
That God has you in His care,
May He fulfill your every dream,
and answer every prayer.

Have a
Wonderful Birthday

> you have everything.
> stay sweet as you are.
> I love you dearly

May 3, 2008

Special Blessing For You on Your Birthday

Dearest Stacey,

I thank God for giving me such a lovely daughter. You are a blessing to the family. I wish I could make your dream come true by giving you your Lexus but you never know what God has in store, but from Him, Jason, Dad, your sister, nephews, aunts and uncles, you have everything.

Stay sweet as you are.

I love you dearly,

Mom

May 2110

Hi Stace
        I can't believe I did not get you a card for your 29th bday. Girl you can tell mom is loosing it.
    I love you & thank god for you always.
        Love.
            Mom
PS. Better late than never.

Lots of love and
Birthday wishes
For more joy than words
can say
To a daughter who adds
sunshine
And a smile to any day!

The god I serve well direct you in the path He wants you to go. Don't be discouraged Hold on. He will never let you go ♥ Mom

May 21, 2010

To a Dear Daughter: Happy Birthday

Hi Stace.

I can't believe I did not get you a card for your 29th b-day. Girl you can tell mom is losing it. I love you and I thank God for you always.

Love, Mom

P.S. Better late than never

The God I serve will direct you in the path He wants you to go. Don't be discouraged. Hold on. He will never let you go

XOX

Mom

Dear Stacey,

You're wished the best
a day can bring —
One that's filled
with everything
That makes it
worth remembering.

Happy, Happy Birthday

From:- Dad & Mom
with all our love.
Be strong in the Lord
and in the power of His
might. Love.

May, 2011

Especially for You on Your Birthday

Dear Stacey

From Dad and Mom with all our love.

Be strong in the Lord and in the power of His might.

Love.

I believe in you,

and I'm here to help you

in any way I can.

I don't promise it will be easy,

but I know you can do it.

Believe In Yourself

Keep aiming for the stars.

Love always
Mom.

For printer

I Believe in You

I believe in you and I am here to help you in any way I can.

I don't promise it will be easy, but I know you can do it.

Believe in yourself.

Keep aiming for the stars.

Love always,

Mom

Hi Sweetie,

I often whisper
"Thank You, Lord"
to heaven up above
For the blessing of a daughter
who's as sweet as you to love.

With Loving Wishes on Your Birthday and Always

Fr: Mum & Dad
Regardless...
you are beautiful and
you are loved deeply
even when you get a...

May 2012

Thank You for My Daughter, Lord

Hi Sweetie,

"I often whisper Thank you Lord to heaven above for the blessing of a daughter who's as sweet as you to love.

With Loving Wishes on Your Birthday and Always."

From Mom and Dad.

Regardless, you are beautiful and you are ours.

Love you dearly

May 16, 2013

In all your ways acknowledge Him and He will direct your paths. Prov. 3:6 To choose Him first, your career then Mr. I cannot say right, because there are too many Mr. wrongs. Keep looking and testing. There is one in the haystack somewhere. I need to be at one of my kids wedding before I croak. Love you always, keep your head up. Glenn

May 16, 2013

For You, Daughter: Wishing You Blessing on Your Birthday

In all your ways acknowledge Him and He will direct your paths (Prov. 3:16) to choose Him first, your career, then Mr. I cannot say right because there are too many Mr. Wrongs.

Keep looking and testing. There is one in the haystack somewhere.

I need to be at one of my kids' weddings before I croak.

Love you. Always keep your head up.

Mom

Dear Stace   May 2014

Dont quit you are very close to your blessings. I know it is not easy, but your God have you in the palm of His hands. He knows when to give you the desires of your heart. Stay strong Hexx get you covered

Be paitent. All he wants you to do is to believe and trust Him
                    Wish I had more to give

May 3, 2014

God Bless You Dear Daughter On Your Birthday

"Delight yourself in the Lord And He shall give you the desires of your heart." - Psalm 37:4

Dear Stace,

Don't quit you are very close to your blessings. I know it's not easy but your God has you in the palm of His hands. He knows when to give you the desires of your heart. Stay strong. He's got you covered. Be patient.

All He wants you to do is to believe and trust Him.

Wish I had more to give.

From Mom

With all my heart,

Love

> Dear Stacey
>   May all your dreams come alive for 2015.
>   Love always.
>   Proud of you.
>   God's richest blessings in all you do. Always put Him first
>   Mom

May 3, 2015

For You, Daughter: Wishing You Blessing on Your Birthday

Dear Stacey,

May all your dreams come alive for 2015.

Love always.

Proud of you.

God's richest in all you do.

Always put Him first.

Mom

May 3/20/16

To my beautiful Princess

Promise you'll never forget

how far you've come...

because it'll help you remember

how far you can go...

I can't find words to express how much I cherish your love, care and support, especially during my diagnosis. This world would be a better place

...and that you'll always

see yourself the way others see you...

because you're *beautiful*

inside and out.

Happy Birthday

if there were more daughters like you, you all going to reach the level God wants you to be. Keep the faith. Love and good health always
MOM.

May 3, 2016

For You, Daughter, on Your Birthday

"Promise you'll never settle for anything less than
    extraordinary…because that is what you deserve
Promise you'll always believe in yourself and the possibilities
    of each dream…because you can do anything
Promise you will never forget how far you have come…
    because it'll help you remember how far you can go."

To my beautiful princess,
I can't find words to express how much I cherish your love,
    care and support, especially during my diagnosis.
This world would be a better place if there were more
    daughters like you. You are going to reach the level God
    wants you to be. Keep the faith.

Love and good health always,

Mom

*This was the last card that my mom gave me
before she passed away.*

The Life & Legacy of Winnifred Berry

September 23, 1940 - July 25, 2016

Winnifred Berry was born at home on Monday, September 23, 1940 in Retirement, Brown's Town, in the parish of St. Ann, Jamaica. She was born to Clifton and Estella McKenzie as the second of eight children. Her father, Clifton, was a hard-working, God-fearing mason and church deacon. Her mother, Estella, was a family-loving, no-nonsense homemaker. Winnie, as she was lovingly called, is survived by four brothers: George McKenzie, Sybert McKenzie, Lascelles McKenzie and Sydney McKenzie. She is also survived by two sisters: Edna McKenzie-David and Terrice McKenzie. There was a third sister, Hyacinth, who passed away shortly after birth. The McKenzie household was a Christian home that instilled in each child the value of family, caring, hard work, and a desire to strive for excellence. They had many joyous times that always included extended family.

Winnifred Berry attended Keith Basic School. For high school, she attended the prestigious York Castle High School in Brown's Town, St. Ann, where she received the second highest grades in her class. Due to limited financial resources, she was not able to further her education, so upon completing high school she entered the workforce to seek a better life for her family, and to help her parents care for her younger siblings. She worked as a postal clerk and a basic school teacher in a neighbouring town before giving birth to her first child, Christine.

Faced with life as a single parent in rural Jamaica, Winnifred then moved to the city, Kingston, Jamaica, in hopes of finding more opportunities to fulfill her dreams of family and education. In Kingston, she worked as a conductress on the Jamaica Omnibus Service from 1968 to 1972, took care of her daughter, and helped her family. There were still limited opportunities for advancement in the city, so when Winnie learned of a Canadian immigration program where she could work as a live-in caregiver and later apply for her daughter to join her in Canada, she jumped at the chance. Winnifred applied for the program and took her first flight to Toronto in 1972 to work with a Canadian family. In 1974, she was joined in Toronto by her daughter and an aunt.

With a new place to call home, Winnie then began to create the life that she had always dreamed of. She had always valued family and education and the next 30 years were spent creating a life that was full of both. She started out by sponsoring her sister and brother to migrate to Canada. She did not settle for having just two family members close by. Every year for approximately 10 years, she sponsored at least two family members to visit Toronto, so that they, too, could share in the opportunities that were there. Her home during the 1970s and 1980s was always full of extended family. Large Sunday breakfasts were mandatory and summer family outings to Centre Island, Niagara Falls, CNE and Ontario Place created wonderful memories for everyone.

Due to her strong Christian family background, Winnifred believed in the institution of marriage and wanted to fulfill another dream, which was to have a traditional, two-parent family. She reconnected with a former neighbour from Kingston, Nigel Berry, and on August 25, 1979, Nigel Berry and Winnifred McKenzie were married in Jamaica. Shortly afterwards, Nigel migrated to Canada, and they became the proud parents of Stacey and Jason Berry.

After leaving her job as a live-in caregiver, Winnie attended school in the evenings and attained her license as a registered practical nurse. Due to the demands of work and family, she was not able to pursue nursing to a higher level; however, over the years, Winnie earned several certifications to enhance her nursing assistant license. She earned a certificate in Administration of Drugs and Wound Care Management. She also completed training in Child Care Management, Teachers' Aid, and TESOL (Teachers of English to Speakers of other Languages).

In 1990, Winnifred noticed that many young students in Toronto were lacking the basic foundations of education—reading, writing and arithmetic. Since she had worked as a basic school teacher in Jamaica, Winnie felt that she could fill that void and decided to open Back to Basics Learning Centre in her home as a Saturday school. The school began as a part-time school, while Winnie continued to work as a registered practical nurse at Toronto General Hospital. When she retired from Toronto General Hospital in 2003, Back to Basics became her full-time passion. The school grew from a handful of students in 1990 to over 200 students during the 25 years that it was in operation.

Winnie lived a good life. She was able to fulfill her dreams of creating a family and community. She was a model and devoted mother and grandmother to her six grandchildren. As a mother, she kept the no-nonsense spirit of her own mother and made sure that her children and grandchildren knew about her faith, went to church and each had a Bible of their own. Their birthdays and Christmas were always remembered with notes of wisdom written in cards, gifts, and one of her delicious cakes. As a wife, Winnie reflected the virtuous woman in Proverbs 31 perfectly. She was a loving and loyal wife to her husband of 36 years. As an educator and legacy builder, Winnie ministered to her students and patients daily. She was a trusted friend who never hesitated to help others. She was a woman of faith committed to church and the teachings of the Bible. Whenever an obstacle was placed in her way, she used her faith and resilience to get through it. She met each day of life with a smile on her face and hope in her heart.

Winnie's life journey took her from the rural countryside of the island of Jamaica to the suburb of a large metropolis in Canada, a journey of over 2,800 km. Along the way, she faced many challenges and also had many triumphs. We enjoyed a beautiful celebration of her life and commemorated these triumphs at her 75th birthday gala in on September 27, 2015.

Her most profound challenge, however, started on January 8, 2016, when she was diagnosed with stage four cancer. The news rocked her entire community from Jamaica, to Toronto, to the United States, to London. Always the one to maintain a hopeful spirit, Winnie ventured into treatment for the illness and remained faithful that she would be divinely healed. She was supported by family and friends during the journey, however, on Monday, July 25, 2016, her journey ended.

As the saying goes: "Gone, but not forgotten." Winnie will forever be remembered as a woman who first and foremost cared for other people. She loved life and loved to share in others' lives, always looking for a way to help or to heal. We have all been touched by Winnie's generosity, her calm, nurturing spirit, and her warm and friendly smile. Although she has left a huge void for all who knew her, she also left endless memories and examples of the true meaning of life. If we are to each think of the overall lesson to be learned from the life of Winnifred Berry, we would see that faith, family and friends are what gives meaning to life. We would also see that Winnie was a shining example of how to live a full life, and whenever we feel sad about losing her we can remember that one thing that we can never lose is the memories that we created with her. Those memories will forever be etched in our hearts.

Eulogy written by Christine Ittai

Endorsements

*"Good friends are better
than pocket money."*

"It is amazing to see *Deeper Reflections* come to light. For years, Stacey has talked about the book of poems that she has been creating since high school, and her hopes of one day getting them published. Well, that day is here and I love how she has blended these deeply thoughtful poems of faith with the wisdom that our mother, Winnifred Berry, passed on to us frequently.
~ *Christine Nya Ittai, M.A., Doctoral Candidate, Educator and Mental Health Counsellor*

"Stacey is an exemplary young lady, who is a shining example for other young women to emulate. She has excelled in her career endeavours, while giving back to the community. I had the pleasure to witness, firsthand, her profound, loving and respectful relationship with her beloved Mom. This anthology of poems is a reflection of Stacey's inner person, which is a profound and inspiring reflection of the beauty of her beloved Mom, Mrs. Winnifred Berry. Congratulations Stacey and continued success."
~ *Margarett R. Best, Former MPP and Ontario Cabinet Minister*

"*Deeper Reflections* teaches us to love what we have, protect what we want and give what we can. My dear friend Winnie was a constant force of compassion filled with hospitality, and encouraged everyone who knew her to never give up."
~ *Jane Metivier*

"Stacey and Winnie are an extended part of my family. Winnie was a strong, loving and committed woman who transformed the lives of everyone who knew her, especially her students. This book captures how Winnie was able to inspire others to shine, spread their wings and fly."
~ *Michelle Brown*

This book is a heartfelt tribute to my dear friend and former co-worker, Winnifred Berry. It takes you on a journey through Winnie's heart, courage, grace, peace and love. She was a beautiful soul who was always there to give of herself. "
~*Merle Miller*

"Stacey is a great example to young people of the Afro-Caribbean diaspora. She has proven herself to be a role model in the community. As a community mentor, she continues to impact lives, family and communities. Stacey has empowered many on her journey. As an emerging author, she shares her journey through writing, which will touch many lives."
~ *Natalee Johnson, Educator, Child and Youth Worker and Advocate, Founder of Passion 4 Dreams*

"This book has inspired and fueled me to stay committed to my continued growth and quest to always live my life with purpose. I am forever grateful to Stacey for sharing this inspirational book of poems with me and the world!"
~ *Juliet Williams, Realtor and Educator*

"This book is a deep reflection of God's image and is made from the template of greatness. Through faith inspired poems, Stacey reveals that our capacity is infinite and creativity is in our DNA. To ensure we live in truth, we must choose to abide in God's creative and innovative power. Only then can we manifest our destiny."
~ *Garnett Manning, Former Brampton City Councillor*

"During your time of quiet reflection, you will feel strengthened as you meditate on these thoughtful devotional truths to inspire and remind you that you are God's unique creation. This book will ignite your faith as it is a valuable resource that brings encouragement, power and enlightenment for anyone who desires to forge a spiritual connection with God."
~ *Leila Springer, The Olive Branch of Hope, Co-Founder*

Spiritual, truthful and uplifting is how I would describe Stacey's anthology of poems. She expresses herself through a style of writing that touches your heart and soul."
~ *Marigrace Galura, Marigrace Accessories, Designer & Founder*

About the Author

Stacey Ann Berry
Author, Speaker and Consultant
Website: staceyannberry.com
Telephone: 416-214-6899

Stacey is the founder and CEO of Bstellar Consulting Group. She is very passionate about giving back to the community. She is a mentor for Inspire North and is an activator with SheEo World. She volunteered for the Heart and Stroke Foundation and interned as a floor director for Rogers TV in Toronto. She has served as a member of the Toronto Board of Health since 2015.

Her passion for writing and conducting informational interviews led her to become an executive reporter and contributor for *Soulful Image* Magazine. She is also contributor for *Where Itz At* magazine, and Bstellar Consulting Group's success tips blog. She designed and taught professional development seminars at Seneca College and facilitated workshops for United Way Toronto & York Region.

Stacey holds a Master of Public Policy Administration and Law degree and an Honours BA from York University. She obtained a diploma in Legal

Administration and a Certificate in Alternative Dispute Resolution from Seneca College. She also completed a Professional Development Internship at The Washington Centre in Washington, D.C.

Stacey received an award for *Outstanding Contribution to Student Experience* from York University Liberal Arts & Professional Studies, the Young Leaders Award from Endless Possibilities of Hope, and was recognized as one of the 100 Accomplished Black Women In Canada. She was named to the Top 100 Black Women to Watch in Canada, nominated by the Women of Essence Global Awards and was featured in Women of Influence.

10% of annual sales will be donated to
The Olive Branch of Hope
(a support group for women
of African ancestry battling cancer)
www.theolivebranch.ca

www.ingramcontent.com/pod-product-compliance
Lightning Source LLC
Chambersburg PA
CBHW052157110526
44591CB00012B/1983